Great Earth Science Projects™

Hands-on Projects About

Changes in the Earth

Krista West

The Rosen Publishing Group's

PowerKids Press™

New York

Some of the projects in this book were designed for a child to do together with an adult.

Published in 2002 by The Rosen Publishing Group, Inc.
29 East 21st Street, New York, NY 10010

First Edition

Book Design: Michael de Guzman
Project Editors: Kathy Campbell, Jason Moring, Jennifer Quasha, Emily Raabe

Photo Credits: p. 4 © PhotoDisc; pp. 6–21 photographs by Cindy Reiman

West, Krista.
 Hands-on projects about changes in the earth / Krista West.
  p. cm. — (Great earth science projects)
 Includes bibliographical references and index.
 ISBN 0-8239-5844-2
 1. Geology—Experiments—Juvenile literature. [1. Geology—Experiments. 2. Experiments.]   I. Title. II. Series.
QE29 .W465 2002
550'.78—dc21
                                                                                          00-01303

Manufactured in the United States of America

Contents

Think About Changes in Earth

Have you ever wondered why rivers bend or how mountains form? Earth is a constantly changing planet. Some changes happen very slowly over time, like the movement of the continents. Others happen suddenly, like an earthquake. You can understand why and how these things happen by learning more about Earth. Deep inside Earth, things are moving and melting all the time. These movements drive some changes on the land and form mountains, volcanoes, oceans, and **trenches**. Winds and water change the surface of Earth by blowing, melting, and pushing land into place.

A volcano is a break in Earth's crust that is formed when hot, liquid rock, called magma, pushes through to the surface.

Examine an Earth-like Egg

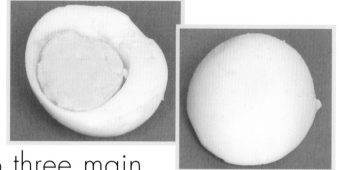

The interior of Earth is divided into three main layers. In the center of our planet is the **core**, or the first layer. The core is a ball of iron, about 2,000 miles (3,219 km) thick. The layer surrounding the core is the **mantle**. The mantle is 1,800 miles (2,897 km) thick and is made of hot, **molten** rock. Movements of the mantle make many of the changes we see on the surface of Earth, such as earthquakes and volcanoes. The **crust**, where we live, is only 3 to 43 miles (5 to 69 km) thick. This solid layer of rock slides on top of the mantle.

You will need
- A hard-boiled egg
- A knife

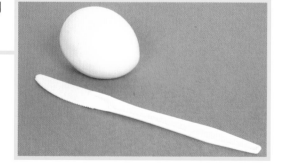

1 Gently crack the shell of a hard-boiled egg but do not remove the shell. Have an adult help you slice it in half lengthwise.

2 Look at the yellow yolk of the egg. The size and shape represent Earth's iron core.

3 Look at the white part of the egg. It surrounds the yolk in the same way that the mantle surrounds Earth's core. However, Earth's mantle is molten, not solid.

4 The eggshell is like Earth's crust. It is very thin compared to the rest of Earth and is broken into many pieces. The bumps and texture of the eggshell are similar to mountains on Earth.

Learn How Plates Move

We live on the outer layer of Earth, called the crust. The crust is broken into many pieces of rock, called **plates**. Plates slide around very slowly on top of molten rock. As the plates slide, the landmasses move around the globe. Even though we can't feel the movements of the plates, we see the effects on the land. Mountains, volcanoes, and earthquakes are all caused by plate movements. The plates move very slowly because the mantle is molten. You can understand why the plates move slowly on the mantle by doing this simple experiment.

You will need

- A casserole dish or a large, shallow bowl
- A spoon
- 3 cups (710 ml) of cornstarch
- 2½ cups (591 ml) of water

Mix the cornstarch and the water in the bowl. It should be a little hard to stir but not dry.

 Slowly stick your fingers in the bowl. What happens? Your fingers should sink in without any problem.

 Pull your fingers out and let the mixture settle until the surface is flat again. Now take your hand and slap the surface of the mixture quickly. What happens? This time your hand shouldn't go in the mixture because you moved quickly.

This mixture acts like Earth's mantle. If you try to move it quickly, it is solid. If you move it slowly, the mixture flows smoothly. The plates riding on Earth's mantle must move slowly for the same reason. If they tried to move quickly, the mantle would be too stiff.

Create Models of Faults

As the plates move around on the surface of Earth, they are constantly pushing and scraping against each other. When this happens, the land changes shape. When two plates are pushed together, the land can buckle to form mountains. Other times, two plates scrape past each other along the edges to form **faults**. A **convergent fault** is when plates push together. At a **divergent fault**, the plates pull away from each other. When plates slide past each other sideways, it's called a **transform fault**. You can make layers of land and experiment with the faults and the land features that they make.

You will need
- 3 colors of clay
- A plastic knife

Flatten each color of clay into a thin circle. Stack these pieces of clay on top of each other.

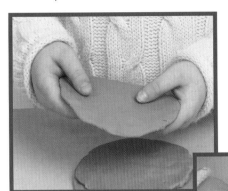

 Place the circles on a table as shown and slowly push the clay until it begins to fold in the middle. This is what happens when plates collide at a convergent fault.

 Cut the clay in half. Slide the two pieces away from each other and notice how a gap forms in the middle. This is called a divergent fault. On Earth, this gap is partially filled by new land from below. This is happening today in eastern Africa.

Now line up the two pieces of clay along the cut sides. Slide one past the other. This is what happens at a transform fault. As the two plates stick and slip, large earthquakes can be generated. This type of motion causes earthquakes in California.

Make a Simple Seismometer

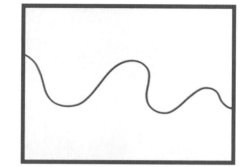

Seismometers are instruments that are used to learn more about the inside of Earth. Earthquakes are caused when a fault moves suddenly or breaks. Scientists don't understand all the details about how earthquakes are **triggered**, but they know how to record them. When an earthquake happens, it sends a wave of energy through Earth, just like a ripple in the water. These waves are recorded with seismometers. You can make your own simple seismometer at home and experiment with energy waves.

You will need

- A felt-tip pen
- A piece of paper
- 6 feet (1.8 m) of string
- Tape
- A doorway
- A chair
- A friend

12

Place a chair in a doorway so that the seat of the chair is directly underneath the door frame.

 Tie a piece of string to the top of the felt tip pen.

 Using tape, hang the pen from the top of the door frame so that the tip just touches the seat of the chair.

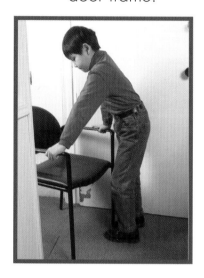

 Put a piece of paper on the seat of the chair underneath the tip of the pen. Have a friend shake the chair slowly while you pull the paper across the seat of the chair. You should get a wave pattern similar to what seismometers record during earthquakes.

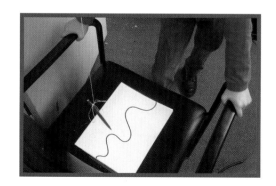

Explore Volcanic Hot Spots

A volcano is a hole in Earth's crust where molten rock and gas rise from the mantle. There are two main places where volcanoes occur. One is near **plate boundaries**, where two pieces of Earth's crust meet and move. The other place where volcanoes occur is called a **hot spot**. It is where molten rock rises through the crust and erupts onto the surface. As the plate moves over the hot spot, new volcanoes are continually formed. The older volcanoes that do not erupt anymore form a long chain of mountains.

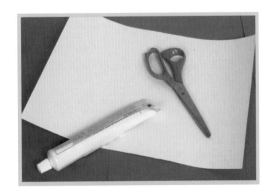

You will need

- An 8½" x 11" piece of poster board
- A pair of scissors
- A large tube of toothpaste
- A friend

1 Carefully poke or cut a line of small holes about 1 inch (2.5 cm) apart in the poster board. Each hole should be about the width of your smallest finger.

2 Open the tube of toothpaste and hold it so that the opening in the tube is pointing toward the ceiling. Do not squeeze it. The toothpaste represents the molten rock that spurts from Earth's mantle.

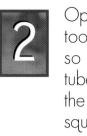

3 Have a friend hold the poster board over the tube of toothpaste so that the first hole lines up with the opening of the tube. The poster board is like Earth's crust. One by one, slowly slide the holes in the poster board over the tube of toothpaste.

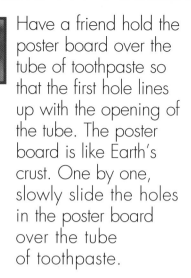

4 At each hole, gently squeeze the tube so that a little bit of toothpaste comes out of each hole as the board moves by. This is how hot spots form chains of islands. As the crust moves over the hot spot, the molten rock rises from the mantle and cools to create mounds of earth.

Discover How Glaciers Shape Earth

One event that shapes Earth's landscape is the movement of **glaciers**. Glaciers form when layers of snow build up in one place and turn into ice. When the piece of ice gets large enough, it begins to move very slowly. Sometimes the glacier gets so big that it runs into nearby land features and pushes them out of the way. Other times Earth's **gravity** pulls the glacier downhill. As the glacier moves, it carves a path and pushes whatever is in its way into a big pile. You can see how glaciers shape Earth in this experiment.

You will need

- 1 cup (237 ml) honey
- ½ cup (118 ml) of sprinkles
- A dinner plate
- A stack of napkins
- 1 tablespoon (14.8 ml) of water

Rest one half of the dinner plate on the stack of napkins. The plate should be at a slight angle.

 Sprinkle a small handful of the sprinkles in a line across the center of the plate. If the sprinkles slide off, try getting the plate slightly wet and then put on the sprinkles.

 Gently pour 1 tablespoon (14.8 ml) of honey onto the elevated side of the plate, covering some of the sprinkles. What happens? The honey may move slightly downhill, but not much. This very slight movement is similar to what happens when a small amount of ice collects in one place on Earth.

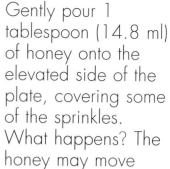

 Pour the rest of the honey over the honey on the plate. This time the honey moves down the plate and pushes some of the sprinkles along as it goes. As a glacier grows, it does a similar thing on Earth. It slowly pushes rocks and debris down a slope.

See Erosion in Action

The shape of a mountain can tell you something about how old it is. This is because of **erosion**. Erosion is the wearing down of land over time. Wind, ice, rain, and moving water can wear down land features such as mountains by stripping away little bits of the dirt and rock. Mountains that are round and smooth probably have been eroding for a long time and are very old. Jagged, pointy mountains probably have not eroded as much. You can see the effects of erosion caused by moving water at home in your kitchen.

You will need

- 3 clear glasses
- 3 pieces of coated candy (like Skittles or M&Ms)
- 2 cups (473 ml) of water
- Tape
- A felt-tip pen
- A piece of paper
- A pair of scissors
- A timer

1 Write a 1, 2, and 3 on the piece of paper. Cut each number out and tape one to each glass. Fill glasses 1 and 2 with 1 cup (237 ml) of water. Leave glass 3 empty.

2 Drop a piece of candy into each glass.

3 Pick up the glass labeled 1 and swirl the candy around in the bottom for about 1 minute. By moving the water around the candy you cause the water to erode the candy. Do this once every 10 minutes for 1 hour. Leave the other two glasses alone.

4 At the end of the hour, compare the candy. The piece in glass 1 will have dissolved much more than those in glasses 2 and 3 because of the erosion you created. Still, water may cause some of the candy to dissolve, but not much. The glass with only air in it will look the same.

Trace the Paths of Rivers

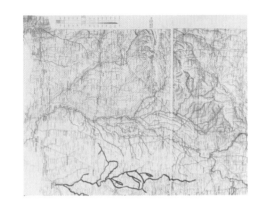

Rivers often change direction, bending and winding their way over Earth. Each river is really the result of a family of smaller rivers, called **tributaries**. Rivers change shape and branch out because the water flowing in them erodes dirt and land as it moves. The flowing water picks up bits of rock and clears the way for more water to flow freely. This process makes **river systems**, or groups of rivers that are connected to each other. You can trace the river systems on a map and see the results of erosion for yourself.

You will need
- A photocopy of a map of some section of the United States
- Orange and blue markers

1 Color a river orange down one side of your map.

 2 You probably will see a lot of small rivers that branch out from or run into the large river. Color those orange, too. These are all part of the same river system.

3 When you're finished coloring in the first river system, begin coloring in the second river. Make it blue. Repeat steps one and two until all the rivers connected to that river are colored. This is a second river system.

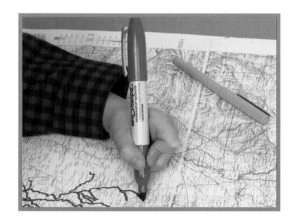

Look Around Your World

Now that you've learned about some of the changes that take place in Earth, like plate movements, faults, volcanoes, glacier movements, and erosion, look around where you live. Are there areas in your environment where there are changes in Earth? If you live near a desert, how might the desert change over time? If you live in a rainy area or wetland, can you see where water has affected the land?

The natural environment where you live was formed by some sort of process. It may have happened quickly. It may have happened slowly. It is probably still happening today. Look around and see what you can learn.

Glossary

convergent fault (kun-VER-jent FAHLT) A place where two plates push together.

core (KOR) The center layer of Earth.

crust (KRUST) The outer layer of Earth that is broken up into many pieces.

divergent fault (dy-VER-jent FAHLT) A place where two plates move away from each other.

erosion (ih-ROH-zhun) The wearing down of land over time.

faults (FAHLTS) Places where two pieces of plates come together.

glaciers (GLAY-shurz) Large masses of ice and rock that move down a mountain or along a valley.

gravity (GRA-vih-tee) The natural force that attracts one object to another.

hot spot (HAHT SPAHT) A place where molten rock constantly reaches Earth's surface.

mantle (MAN-tuhl) The middle layer of Earth that lies between the core and the crust.

molten (MOHL-ten) Something that is made liquid by heat.

plates (PLAYTS) The moving pieces of Earth's crust.

plate boundaries (PLAYT BOUN-dreez) Where two pieces of Earth's crust meet and move.

river systems (RIH-ver SIS-tehmz) Groups of connected rivers all stemming from the same source.

seismometers (syz-MAH-meh-terz) Instruments used to measure movements in Earth.

transform fault (TRANZ-form FAHLT) A place where two plates slide past each other.

trenches (TREN-chez) Deep cracks in the ocean floor.

tributaries (TRIH-byuh-tehr-eez) Rivers that flow into another river or body of water.

triggered (TRIH-gerd) Started.

Index

C
convergent fault, 10
core, 6
crust, 6, 8, 14

D
divergent fault, 10

E
earthquake(s), 5, 6, 8, 12
erosion, 18, 22

F
faults, 10, 22

G
glacier(s), 16, 22

M
mantle, 6, 8
molten rock, 6, 8, 14
mountains, 5, 8, 10, 14, 18

P
plate(s), 8, 10, 14, 22

R
rivers, 5, 20

T
transform fault, 10
tributaries, 20

V
volcanoes, 5, 6, 8, 14, 22

Web Sites

To learn more about changes in Earth, check out these Web sites:
http://kids.earth.nasa.gov
http://quake.wr.usgs.gov